TRIUMPH
BONNEVILLE T140

& Derivatives
1973 - 1988

Roy Bacon

First published in the United Kingdom by:
Niton Publishing
PO Box 3. Ventnor. Isle of Wight PO38 2AS

Acknowledgements
The author would like to thank those who
helped this book by supplying the photographs. Most came from the EMAP archives
or *Motor Cycle News* by courtesy of the
editor, Malcolm Gough, with some
from the author's files.

This edition published 1995 by
The Promotional Reprint Company Ltd,
exclusively for Selecta Book Limited,
Roundway, Devizes, Wiltshire SN10 2HR
and Reed Editions in Australia.

ISBN 1 85648 305 3

Printed in Hong Kong

A 1978 T140 Bonneville in its home market finish and out on the road.

Contents

Introduction

The Triumph T140 Bonneville was developed from the older T120 version in 1973 by increasing the capacity. This rose from 649 to 725 cc at first, and then to 744 cc. To go with the Bonneville, there was the single-carburettor Tiger 750, and these two machines carried the firm through the trauma of the Meriden sit-in of the mid-1970s.

With this behind them, the firm expanded its range into the 1980s by introducing variations on the Bonneville theme. These included a couple of trail models, a smaller-capacity economy twin and, finally, two 600 twins. Machines were built in alternative styles for the UK and USA markets in most years and, later on, in custom form to suit that segment of the market.

There were also a couple of interesting proto-types during this era and some technical innovation. Even police sales were not forgotten in the search for business, for Triumph had built up a very successful rapport with many forces in the post-war years.

In the end, the Meriden plant had to close, but the name continued in Devon for another few years. Production finally ceased in 1988, but who can be certain of that, for the Triumph twin, born late in 1937, so often returned to the market place after its death had been reported!

The 1979 Bonneville Special, with its siamesed exhaust system and cast-alloy wheels, outside the Meriden factory and fitted with the USA tank and bars.

Bonneville and Tiger

The Bonneville and Tiger 750 were twin- and single-carburettor versions of the same motorcycle, so the differences were minimal. Other than the cylinder head, inlet manifold and extra carburettor, the only differences were the air filter boxes and the petrol tank and side panel decor.

Both models had a five-speed gearbox built in unit with the engine, and the construction followed the lines set by the first 649 cc unit twins of 1963. The basis was a cast-alloy crankcase with a vertical split that ran on the engine centre-line to the rear of the crankcase and then stepped over to the left. This enabled the whole of the gearbox housing to be part of the right-hand casting, while the left-hand case included the primary chaincase inner.

Engine mountings were cast-in at the front, rear and under-side. The rear one was a lug above the gearbox sprocket, one part being formed as an extension of the chaincase, above and to its rear, and the other a casting that ran up from the gear-

First of the T140V line was this 1973 model which has the UK tank but the USA style silencers.

For the USA there were raised bars, a smaller tank and no fork gaiters as seen on this T140V of 1973.

box shell roof. These two sections combined to enclose the area over the sprocket and rear chain to keep dirt at bay. Access to the sprocket and its nut was via a circular door fitted to the chaincase inner, and an oil seal fitted in this door ran on the gearbox mainshaft.

The engine was laid out in typical Triumph twin fashion, so the crankshaft ran in two main bearings - a ball race on the timing side and a roller on the drive. The camshafts were positioned fore and aft of the crankshaft and high in the crankcase where they ran in plain bushes. They were driven by gears, a pinion on the right-hand crankshaft end being meshed with an intermediate gear mounted on a fixed spindle pressed into the crankcase wall. This gear drove both camshaft gears, and

all were marked to assist in setting the valve timing.

The crankshaft had an 82 mm stroke and was forged in one with a separate flywheel. This was fitted to the centre web and held in place by three radial bolts. A sludge trap was formed within the crankpins, and an oil tube was fitted within this and retained by a screwed plug. Each connecting rod had a split big-end with replaceable shell bearings, and its cap was retained and located by two bolts with self-locking nuts.

Each three-ring piston was attached to its connecting rod by a gudgeon pin that was retained by wire circlips. The compression ratio was 8.25:1 and, at first, the pistons ran in 75 mm bores, which gave a 725 cc capacity. After a short while, these figures were increased

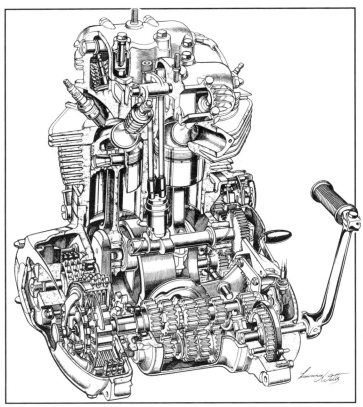

The 744 cc
Bonneville engine
and gearbox unit
which could trace
its roots back to the
1937 Speed Twin.

to 76 mm and 744 cc, where they were to stay. The pistons ran in a one-piece, cast-iron block that had individual cylinder spigots running down into the crankcase, to which it was held by eight studs with nuts, four of the latter being of the 12-point type.

A gasket went under the block, which had holes fore and aft on its centre-line for tappet guide blocks. Each of these carried two tappets with radiused feet and, once pressed into place, was retained by a set bolt. A chrome-plated pushrod tube,

with suitable seals, was fitted over each tappet block and ran up into the underside of the cylinder head to enclose the pushrods.

The one-piece cylinder head was an aluminium casting, held down to the block by ten bolts, with a gasket between the two. Each pair of valves, exhausts at the front and inlets at the rear, had its own well, to which a light-alloy rocker box was bolted. The valves operated in guides, which were pressed in to a shoulder, and were controlled by duplex coil springs sitting in cups and retained by collars and split collets.

Each rocker box had two one-piece, forged rockers mounted on a common fixed spindle, and there was an array of thrust and spring washers to absorb wear and control end-float. The spindles were hollow and supplied with lubricating oil from one end. Each rocker had a ball-end pressed into its inner arm, and an adjuster screw and locknut in the outer to set the valve clearance. A single finned lid on each rocker box gave access to the adjusters and was held in place by four screws.

The Bonneville and Tiger had common detail parts for their engine top halves, except for the cylinder heads themselves. The T140V, for example, had four studs in a row, on the inlet side, to carry its twin

Amal Concentric 930 carburettors and their inlet tracts. The tracts were linked by a flexible balance pipe, and the left-hand tract also carried a bracket for the air lever. For the Tiger, there was an inlet manifold for a single 930 carburettor, and this was held by two pairs of vertically disposed studs. On the exhaust side, the pipes simply pushed into place, this arrangement having appeared in the previous year on the T120 to replace the screwed-in stubs of old.

Dry-sump lubrication was used, with a twin-plunger oil pump being mounted in the timing chest where it was driven by an offset pin on the inlet camshaft gear nut. The system pressure was controlled by a release valve fitted in the front of the right-hand crankcase, below the

The single carburettor version of the twin was the Tiger 750 and this is the 1973 model for the USA.

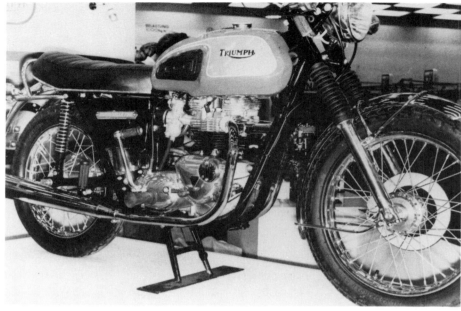

The home market T140V of 1973 on show when it still had its gear pedal on the right.

timing chest. The oil was then fed into the timing cover, and from this into the right-hand end of the crankshaft to lubricate the big-ends.

Oil was also taken, via a hollow dowel, to the exhaust tappets and their guide block, but the rocker feed was from the oil return line. A pressure switch in the front of the timing cover was connected to a warning light to alert the rider of any problem with the system. The return pump was protected by a filter screwed into the underside of the right-hand crankcase in the sump area, but the feed pump filter was external.

Engine breathing was via holes into the primary chaincase, which was vented from the top rear corner. An elbow was bolted to the rear of the casting and a flexible pipe connected to this. The assembly within the chaincase included a catchment with a pipe to carry oil directly on to the primary chain.

The electrics were based on a 12 volt system, the battery being charged by an RM21 alternator mounted on the left-hand end of the crankshaft within the primary chaincase. Its output was controlled by a zener diode with a rectifier to convert it to direct current. Ignition was by twin coils, two sets of contact points being mounted in the timing cover. Their cam and its auto-advance were driven from the end of the exhaust camshaft, and a small cover enclosed the assembly.

A rev-counter drive was taken from the left-hand end of the exhaust camshaft, with a drive box fixed to the crankcase and the flexible cable connected to this.

The engine drove the five-speed gearbox via a triplex primary chain and a multi-plate clutch. The engine sprocket was splined to the crankshaft inboard of the alternator rotor, so the stator was mounted on three studs to provide chain clearance. The chain itself was tensioned by a blade under its lower run, and the adjuster for this emerged low down at the rear of the chaincase. The chaincase outer was fixed to the inner by a row of screws and the joint sealed with a gasket; a screwed plug on the gearbox mainshaft centre-line acted as a filler and gave access to the adjuster screw in the clutch pressure plate. A round cover, held by three screws, went on the crankshaft centre-line, and its removal enabled the ignition timing to be checked with a strobe light. To assist with this, the rotor was marked and a timing pin fitted to the chaincase.

The clutch was a conventional Triumph type with a shock absorber built into its central hub. The clutch drum, with the triple-row sprocket, ran on free rollers and drove the six driving plates, which had bonded-

Police versions of the Triumph twin were sold as the 750 Saint, an acronym for 'stops anything in no time'.

on inserts. The six plain plates drove the centre hub, the spider of which was splined to the inner hub mounted on the gearbox mainshaft. The plates were clamped by three compression springs, and the pressure plate had the adjuster screw and locknut at its centre.

The gearbox and its five-speed cluster were of typical British layout, the mainshaft being above the layshaft and concentric with the sleeve gear. This last was supported in a roller bearing and had two needle-roller races fitted in its bore to carry the mainshaft. A ball race went at the right-hand end of the mainshaft, while the layshaft had a needle race at each end.

The gears were selected by a trio of forks, all mounted on one rod, which were controlled by a circular cam-plate. This had a small pinion fitted to it, which meshed with a quadrant that was moved by the positive-stop mechanism; this culminated at a gear pedal on the right, which was ahead of the kickstart lever. The latter had a folding pedal and was fixed by cotter to a spindle

The 1976 Tiger 750 with left gear pedal and disc rear brake, changes brought about by legislation in the USA.

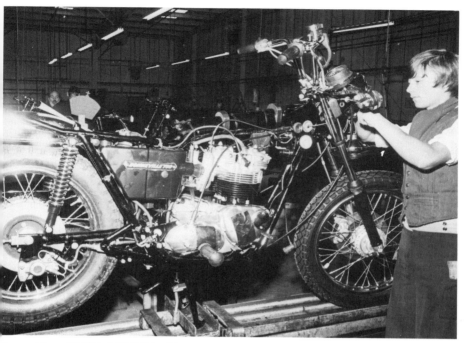

Assembling a T140V of 1976-77 at Meriden and the handlebars indicate a USA build model. It is near the end of the line.

carrying a quadrant gear at its inner end, which meshed with a pinion on the right-hand end of the mainshaft. The pinion incorporated a face ratchet so that it could turn the engine over and then return the quadrant with the help of a clock spring.

The positive-stop and kickstart mechanisms were fitted into the space between the inner and outer gearbox covers. The inner carried the gearbox bearings, while the outer supported the pedal shafts and was formed to blend in with the timing cover ahead of it. The space between the covers also housed the clutch lift mechanism, which was of the ball-and-ramp type. In this, the cable moved the carrier of three ball bearings so that they ran up ramps to give movement to the pushrod and pressure plate.

The engine and gearbox unit was mounted in an oil-carrying frame, which had first been adopted by the group in 1971. It was based on a single massive tube that formed the top and seat tube, as well as the oil tank. To this end, there was a filler cap in the top tube near the bend, pipe attachments as required, and a filter at the bottom of the seat tube. Thus, the filter and its mounting plate formed the base of the oil tank. The rest of the frame consisted of

TRIUMPH T140 BONNEVILLE

The 1976 TR7V Tiger 750 with its single carburettor which made it easier to keep running evenly.

duplex downtubes, which ran on under the engine and then up to the tops of the rear suspension units. At this point, they joined the dualseat loop, which was attached to the main frame tube and also ran back to support the rear mudguard. Additional loops held the silencers and pillion rests, while cross-members braced the frame.

The pivoted rear fork was a welded tubular assembly, its fork legs extending ahead of the cross-member joining them. They carried the bushes on which the fork moved, and there were sleeves on a fixed spindle for the bushes to bear on. The spindle was fitted into plates

Timing side of a 1977 Bonneville T140V with its typical Triumph line that was never to be lost.

that were welded to each of the duplex frame tubes, and it also ran through a cross-tube welded to the rear of the seat tube. Thus, the fork pivots straddled the centre tube and were supported by the outer plates.

Girling rear units with hydraulic damping and 110 lb/in. plated used to protect the stanchions on home market machines, but were omitted from those sent to the USA. The fork legs were in polished light alloy, each wheel spindle cap being held in place on four studs. The fork top yoke was fitted with a steering lock and two rubber bushes for the

Show time with a 1977 T140V Bonneville fitted with special wheels.

springs were used, without any spring covers. The frame carried the engine unit in frame lugs and rear mounting plates, with a head steady at the top, and was completed by centre and prop stands.

Telescopic front forks with internal springs and hydraulic damping were fitted. They turned in taper-roller head races, and gaiters were eyebolts that held the handlebars. A steering damper was available as an option, the friction discs being mounted below the bottom yoke and the control knob above the steering stem nut.

Covers went over the legs between the yokes and were black for the home market, but chrome-plated for the USA. Each carried a head-

TRIUMPH T140 BONNEVILLE

The Jubilee Bonneville as built for the USA with high bars and small tank in 1977.

lamp bracket with a rubber mounting between the parts to reduce the effects of engine vibration. The left-hand bracket provided a mounting for the ignition switch and, with the right-hand one, supported a chrome-plated headlamp shell. The fixings

for this also acted as the mounting stalks for the front turn signals, while the shell had a toggle switch for the lights, together with warning lamps in red, green and amber, mounted in it.

Although the first photographs

Each Jubilee carried this legend on its side panels and was issued with a numbered certificate.

Home market Jubilee T140 with its more restrained looks which suited the occasion so well.

of the T140 show it with a conical front hub and drum brake, the production machine had a disc front brake of 10 in. diameter. The hub of the front wheel was in two halves, which were held together by four bolts that also held the disc to them. The assembly was spoked into a steel rim fitted with a 3.25 x 19 in. tyre.

The brake disc went on the left-hand side of the wheel and was arrested by a twin-pad caliper bolted to the fork leg. The master cylinder,

complete with fluid reservoir, was clamped to the handlebars and connected to the caliper by a combination of rigid and flexible pipes.

At the rear, the 1971 design wheel with conical hub was fitted. This hub was in light alloy, with the rear wheel sprocket bolted to it, and included the speedometer drive gearbox. It was not quickly detachable. The hub incorporated a 7 in. single-leading-shoe drum brake, with a torque arm to anchor the backplate, and this was operated by a pedal on the left. Again, the hub was spoked into a steel rim, which was fitted with a 4.00 x 18 in. tyre.

Both front and rear mudguards were chrome-plated and of blade section. The support for the rear one included a mounting for the

home and general export machines having a new, slimline part with a long, slow-taper megaphone ending in a curved reverse-cone end. For the USA, older megaphone silencers were fitted in the style used on the T120 from 1971.

The 1977 Bonneville as built for the USA with bars and tank, including its finish style, to suit.

rear turn signals and a handrail behind the hinged dualseat. A large tail-light was fitted to a support mounted on the rear mudguard, just above the rear number plate.

The exhaust pipes had a balance pipe to connect them close to the ports, and were common to all markets. The silencers varied, the

The air cleaner assembly comprised left- and right-hand body and cover plastic mouldings, which fitted together to enclose an air filter element on each side of the machine. The parts were arranged so that either twin rubber hoses connected the assembly to the twin carburettors of the Bonneville, or a

Rather nice Bonneville T140V modified to café racer style and on show at Belle Vue in 1977.

single rubber moulding joined it to the sole instrument of the Tiger. Covers to the rear of the air cleaner assembly, on each side of the machine, filled in the corners of the subframe. These carried suitable badges to inform the world as to the model, while the battery and electrics went behind them.

The petrol tank for USA machines held three gallons and was fitted with 'frame' type tank badges. The

A 1978 Bonneville at a show and most likely being handed over as a prize.

TRIUMPH T140 BONNEVILLE

The TR7V made a good sidecar machine and a 1978 model is seen here hitched up and ready to go.

tank decoration and colour varied between models, the Bonneville being in Hi-Fi Vermilion and gold, while the Tiger was in Astral blue and opal. For the home market, a four gallon tank with slab sides was fitted, and this carried basic 'Triumph' badges. The colours were as for the USA, but the styling was not, being altered to suit the different tank shape.

The controls had the minor electrical ones built into the lever housings, but they were unmarked and none too easy to use. Both speedometer and rev-counter instrument

heads were held in rubber cups mounted in flat ring plates. These, in turn, were held by large bolts, listed as cap nuts, which were threaded into the true fork cap nuts, one on each side.

This completed the two models, which were only coloured on their petrol tanks, the rest of the machines being chrome-plated, polished or in black. They received a good welcome, for the extra capacity helped the performance and the way in which it was delivered, while the disc brake had become accepted practice and was really overdue.

Meriden sit-in and aftermath

By the early 1970s, the British motorcycle industry was in disarray, with few major firms left, although a number of small concerns continued in the competition market. The industry really comprised BSA, Norton and Triumph, the last being owned by BSA anyway.

By then, Norton had switched all of its production to variants of their Commando with its unique Isolastic engine mounting system. BSA and Triumph had together staged a major group launch late in 1970 to introduce both new and revamped models with either marque badge. Much of this work came from the infamous group research centre at Umberslade Hall, which produced a frame with an excessively high seat height for both BSA and Triumph twins in 1971.

There were many other mistakes, both technical and managerial, with

The T140E version of the Bonneville came in for 1978 and this is one in the USA trim, ready to cope with the emission limits.

Another show
picture and this
time of a 1978
Tiger 750 and a kilt.

the result that many new models failed to go into production. Others, such as the Ariel 3, did appear, but were a total flop and cost the group dearly. The basic models, including the twins, suffered less, as both BSA and Triumph kept to their existing and well tried engine and gearbox units.

New for the twins, and some singles, were the forks and hubs, while the oil-bearing frame was built in forms to suit singles and twins. It was the twin version that was later used by the T140, along with the group forks and rear hub, air cleaner housings, side covers and other detail parts, some with minor alterations.

One of the problems caused by the new design of cycle parts was that the new drawings were late. This brought the Triumph plant to a halt in the autumn of 1970, and when the factory was finally able to tool-up and start production, it was found that the engine would not fit into the frame. At this point, any regard Meriden had for the team at Umberslade, or the group's management, vanished, never to return.

Desperate work at Meriden enabled assembly to start and, in time, even the excessive seat height was reduced to a more acceptable level. In this way, the T120 ran on and later became the T140. Meanwhile, BSA stumbled towards financial disaster. Innumerable rescue plans were tabled, and Dennis Poore, the chairman of Norton Villiers, was asked by the government to become involved and come up with an answer before the bank brought in a receiver.

The outcome was the formation of Norton Villiers Triumph, or NVT, in the summer of 1973. This was given financial support by the government, and a variety of company names appeared at the different sites owned by the group. For the workforce at Meriden, the future looked good, for they thought that Triumph production would stay at

This 1979 photo shows a Bonneville used as the basis of an experimental safety machine with leg protectors and chest restraint.

TRIUMPH T140 BONNEVILLE

Many choppers used the big Triumph twin engine unit to power them and this typical example was seen at Brands Hatch in 1989.

their plant, while the Umberslade interference was no longer present and, in the meantime, they had their annual holiday to enjoy.

The return to the works was marred by a minor dispute, but this was soon dealt with. The shop stew-

ards then requested a meeting with Dennis Poore, with a view to confirming the position and seeing the man face-to-face. It was scheduled for a mid-September Friday, but on the day rumours circulated that Meriden was to close. At lunchtime,

The timing side of the T140E Bonneville in 1979, set against a pleasant background.

The T140E Bonneville drive side in 1979, again in a nice location.

the local paper confirmed this, leaving the workforce devastated, baffled and then extremely angry.

This, they felt, was the result of several years' interference, and they just refused to accept the decision. So they took over the plant and the Meriden sit-in began. It went on for 18 months and became a political pawn, for the general election of early 1974 had returned a Labour government, and left-winger Tony Benn became the minister involved. After considerable discussion a workers co-operative was set up.

The sit-in finally ended in March 1975, but even then there were con-

tinual complications with money, organisation, the marketing and sales structure and cash flow. Eventually, the rights to all aspects of the business were returned to Meriden in 1977, but this still left the firm and its workforce with a hard slog to keep going and carry out any developments.

Due to all these problems, the 1974 models had no real life at all, but at least they did exist, although often as work-in-progress for a considerable time. Changes were minimal, with just two extra screws for each rocker box cover, the removal of the steering damper, even as an option, and a few detail amendments. The tank colours became Cherokee red for the Bonneville and Sea Jade for the Tiger, both combined with Ice white.

The last 1974 models were completed in early 1975, when the sit-in ceased, and from April that year to June, machines to the same specifi-

T140V Bonneville and TR7V Tiger, having the same differences as before in the number of carburettors and the effect of this on the associated parts. The change to the left-foot gearchange was achieved by connecting the positive-stop mechanism to a shaft that ran across the crankcase to the pedal outside the

Bonneville T140E in USA build form on show to promote the new carburettors used to meet the legal requirements.

cation were built as 1975 models. From July on, production was of 1976 machines, which were revised to a left-foot gearchange and disc rear brake. This change was dictated by new USA legislation, and the necessary design work had taken place during the sit-in to enable the alterations to be incorporated as soon as the existing parts stock had been used up.

The two models were built as the

primary chaincase. The shaft included a stirrup to get round the clutch, and the new outer chaincase had a small screwed cap to give access for checking the ignition timing with a strobe. This replaced the earlier, larger cover held by three screws.

The rear wheel hub was new and had a 10 in. brake disc, but the rim and tyre remained as before. The brake caliper hung below the right-

The 1979 T140D Bonneville Special in its home market form with low bars and large petrol tank but fitted with stock exhaust system.

side rear fork leg and wheel spindle, the pads being moved by hydraulic pressure from a master cylinder. This was linked to the brake pedal on the right-hand side of the ma- chine. Other changes comprised revised ends for the silencers, and built-in switches for both sides of the handlebars, while the T140 tank colours were red or blue with white

A police version of the Triumph twin in 1980 with special fairing and lights. This business was useful to the firm for many years.

Police Bonneville on show in April 1981 with Transport Minister Norman Fowler talking to Triumph

side panels and those of the TR7V jade green and white.

The two machines continued as they were for 1977, when they were joined by the Jubilee version of the Bonneville. This was built in celebration of the 25 years that Queen Elizabeth had reigned and was a limited edition model, 1000 being built for the USA, 1000 for the home market, and 400 for other countries. Each one came with a certificate of authenticity.

The Jubilee was standard as regards specification, except that the tyre sizes became 4.10 x 19 in. front, and 4.10 x 18 in. rear, Dunlop Red Arrow covers being fitted. It was in the finish that the model was special, red, white and blue on silver being used for the petrol tank, mudguards, side covers and rear chainguard. The wheel rims were chrome-plated with blue centres, lined in white and red, while the primary chaincase and timing cover were chrome-plated. The seat was in Powder blue with red piping, and the whole effect was stunning, but dignified, as befitted the occasion.

Only the two standard models continued for 1978, and they had limited alterations. Included in these was a halogen headlight bulb and Veglia instruments on some machines, the latter depending on Smith's supply problems. The dualseat was new and made with wide or narrow nose sections, to suit the tanks, as well as in two colours to match the finish. The machine colour was extended to include the mudguards and side panels, there being a choice of aquamarine and silver or Tawny brown and gold. For the USA, the mudguards continued with the chrome-plated finish.

Emission control

One further model was introduced for 1978 and listed as the T140E to signify that it had complied with the regulations on emission control in the USA. Without this, it could not have been sold in that market, which was essential to the firm. Meeting the requirements was not easy and involved lengthy and, thus, expensive tests, which were hard for a small company to cope with.

To meet the emission levels, a new cylinder head with parallel inlet ports was introduced. This enabled the twin carburettors to have a common choke lever. The instruments fitted were Amal Mark 2 Concentrics with a cold-start system, rather than the airslide and tickler of the past. These measures enabled the engine to run on a leaner mixture and, thus, meet the test levels.

Road testing a 1980 Bonneville, the year the electric start was introduced.

Nice picture of a 1980 Bonneville with electric start out in use with tank bag and panniers for the luggage.

The T140E was available in three colours, the Tawny brown and gold tank finish being matched by brown side panels and dualseat. The other colours were Astral blue and silver, or Candy Apple red and black, both side panels and seat being black in these cases.

This work left little time or effort available for much else, but there were changes for 1979, when the T140E replaced the older Bonneville completely, while the TR7V continued. Both were fitted with electronic ignition, the trigger for which went in the former points housing.

The drive continued to be from the exhaust camshaft, but without the auto-advance, as this was carried out electronically, and the ignition trigger was enclosed by a new finned cover. The alternator was changed to a three-phase Lucas RM24 with the appropriate rectifier, but the rotor and stator interchanged with the older components.

There were new handlebar switches of improved design, and a small console appeared between the instruments. It carried four warning lights, the additional one being for neutral. The whole layout was much improved by these changes. A rear carrier was added above the rear light mounting, and the tyre sections changed to the 4.10 in. used by the Jubilee, although the wheel diameters were unaltered. Both the Bonneville and the Tiger continued to be offered in UK and USA forms, which affected the handlebar rise and petrol tank style and capacity.

During 1979, the range was extended by the addition of the T140D Bonneville Special. This was mainly a styling exercise, for the stock engine, frame and forks were used with cast-alloy Lester wheels. Both kept the single disc brake, but the rear caliper was moved to a position

above the wheel centre so that it was further out of any spray thrown up by the wheel in wet weather. A two-into-one exhaust system was fitted, the pipes tucking in to join under the front of the crankcase and then run to the single silencer mounted low down on the right of the machine. The T140D was equipped with a two-level dualseat and, for the USA, a lean, two-gallon petrol tank. The finish was dramatic in black with gold tank and side cover lining, chrome-plated mudguards, and a black finish to the insides of the alloy wheel spokes.

The three models ran on for 1980 with an improved oil pump and the

Close up of a 1980 T140ES engine to show the installation of the starter motor and new timing cover to enclose the drive gears.

TRIUMPH T140 BONNEVILLE

revised rear brake caliper as used on the T140D. Exhaust systems were tucked in a little more, and quite a range of colours was offered for the petrol tank and side covers. Machines for the USA continued to have high-rise handlebars and small tanks with their own paint style, but the colour range was similar for both markets.

The T140D continued in its black with gold lining, but the home market T140E was available in metallic grey with Candy Apple red panels or black with white lining. For the USA, the T140E was listed in grey with black flashes, black with Candy

Apple red flashes or Olympic Flame with black. The TR7V was only built for its home market and Europe with a silver blue sheen finish, set off with gold and dark blue lining.

Thus, Triumph seemed to have put its problems behind it and, in fact, had enjoyed good sales for a year or two, plus taking the important *Motor Cycle News* 'Machine of the Year' title in 1979. The twins had their own niche in the market, and comparisons with other vertical twins often rather missed the point. It was not the actual performance that mattered, but the way in which it was delivered.

This is the Low Rider T140PE Phoenix shown by the firm in August 1980 to gauge rider's reactions to the style.

The 1981 T140 Executive Bonneville with the additional side fairing sections available as an option. Screen, panniers, cockpit fairing and top box were fitted as standard.

The company seemed set fair for the 1980s, but then the pound strengthened against the dollar, which forced up prices of the machines in the USA. Sales fell off badly and, once again, the workforce was struggling. By then, the firm's debt was 12 million pounds and rising by another million every three months.

The workforce was cut and plans laid to move into a smaller plant to reduce the crippling rates bill, but this proved impossible.

Despite the problems, the firm tried to keep its range moving forward, and the 1980s were to bring a number of new variants on the old and familiar twin theme.

New ranges

The first change for the new decade came in the middle of 1980, when an electric-start option was offered for all models. The starter motor was tucked in behind the block, in the old magneto position, and drove a train of gears in the timing chest. A new timing cover enclosed the drive and had a section that could be removed to provide access to the motor fixings.

When the starter was fitted, the

For the 1981 Paris show the firm produced the TR7T Tiger Trail with this waist level exhaust system.

In production the Tiger Trail had a different exhaust with low pipe and angled silencer on the left.

main model became the T140ES and had the word 'Electro' on its side panels. This re-typing was not done for the TR7V and T140D, which were to be short-lived anyway and would disappear from the range early in 1981.

Before then, in July 1980, the Executive Bonneville was added to the line-up. This was based on the T140ES with the addition of a Sabre cockpit fairing by Brealey-Smith, and panniers and top box from Sigma. The custom finish was in a deep maroon, which shaded into ruby with gold lining. The model was shown to press and public during TT week that year.

In August 1980, Triumph presented their 1981 range at a London show. It included a new version called the T140PE Phoenix. This was in the low rider mould, the frame being amended to lower the riding position, and fitted with laid-down rear units and a fat, 5.10 x 16 in. rear tyre. The dualseat was stepped in chopper style, while the forks were extended and the front tyre was a slim 3.00 x 19 in. The engine was the T140E unit, but with splayed inlet ports, although the Mark 2 Concentrics remained. The handlebars were high and the petrol tank small. The machine was shown to evaluate interest and judge whether or not to put it into production.

For the other models, there were internal engine improvements, exhaust pipes that were clamped into the ports, and a better alternator and control system. Options for the T140E included cast wheels, now by Morris, as the Lester type became difficult to obtain, two-into-one exhaust, dual front discs, the cockpit fairing and the electric starter. The wheels, dual discs and exhaust became available for the T140ES, while all these were available for the Executive, together with a full fairing option, achieved by bolting lower side panel mouldings to the cockpit one.

Late in 1980, the firm had most of their debt to the government written off and ceased to be a co-operative. They became a limited company with directors, while the workforce became shareholders. The good news about the debt encouraged them to put together a

new model for the Paris show, and this was introduced as the TR7T Tiger Trail. It was much in the style of the old Trophy model, with a detuned, single-carburettor engine in the stock frame and forks, these last being fitted with gaiters. The front wheel retained its disc brake, but was fitted with a 3.00 x 21 in. tyre and rim to suit. At the rear, the tyre was a 4.00 x 18 in. size, but the hub went back to a 7 in. drum brake.

The fixtures and fittings were to suit the off-road or trail use, there being plastic mudguards, a short dualseat, undershield and braced bars. The exhaust system was finished in matt black, and the siamesed pipes ran into a waist-level silencer on the left on the show model. Later, the single pipe ran under the primary chaincase to a si-

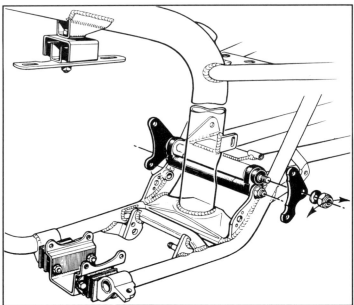

Line drawing of the anti-vibration mounting system devised for Triumph by Bernard Hooper.

lencer that ran up and back, before extending to the rear. The tank, side covers and mudguards were in a bright yellow, so the model stood out well.

One of the major drawbacks of any vertical twin is the vibration the engine generates, and firms tried various ways of counteracting the effects. One method was the 180-degree crankshaft, which met with partial success, while another was to add a balancer shaft driven by the engine. This produced a second series of vibrations, and it was feasible for the two sets to cancel out

The basic Bonneville continued with options and this 1981 T140ES has the cast-alloy wheels and dual front brake discs.

The 649 cc TR65 Thunderbird introduced for 1981 with a number of price cutting features and here in its USA form.

each other as far as the rider was concerned. The forces still existed, of course, and the crankcase had to be designed to cope with them.

Yet another method was the Isolastic system used by Norton for their Commando twins and designed by Bernard Hooper. Triumph de-

The engine unit of the Thunderbird had a matt black finish for the covers, a single carburettor and points ignition.

Home market version of the Thunderbird with the drum rear brake common to this budget model.

cided to follow that route, as the changes and costs were low, and Hooper came up with a new system for them. With this, the engine and gearbox unit was rubber mounted, so it could move vertically within limits imposed by rubber blocks. The rear engine plates carried the pivoted rear fork and were linked to the frame, so the whole assembly stayed in line, but could move to a limited extent.

The first machines with anti-vibration mounts went to the police, who needed them more than most on their long shifts and who would provide the essential feedback on the system. The police models were based on the Bonneville with the extra fairing, panniers and police equipment, as usual, plus twin front discs to cope with the added weight.

In April 1981, there was a further UK show, which brought changes to the Triumph model range. The TR7V was dropped, as was the T140D, although it was still feasible to arrive at the latter by using the option list.

TRIUMPH T140 BONNEVILLE

There was considerable interest in the TS8-1 when it went on show in 1981 but it never went into production in this form.

This left the T140E, T140ES and Executive Bonneville, the last being fitted with twin Bing carburettors in place of the Amals. The TR7T continued and was joined by a new model, which revived an old name.

The new machine was the 649 cc TR65 Thunderbird, and the reduced capacity was obtained by shortening the stroke of the stock Bonneville engine to 71.5 mm. This meant a new crankshaft and shorter block, while points ignition and a black engine finish were both adopted to

The limited edition Royal Bonneville was built in celebration of the marriage between Prince Charles and Lady Di, this being the home market version.

reduce costs on this budget model. There was only a single Amal 930 carburettor, and costs were further cut with a 7 in. drum rear brake and matt black, siamesed exhaust system with the silencer low down on the left.

A second new model was at the show, and this was the TS8-1, which had an eight-valve engine mounted in the anti-vibration frame. The new cylinder head was based on Weslake and Nourish conversions, but was to run into problems when finally produced by Triumph. The machine itself had advanced styling by Ian Dyson and featured a full fairing

and twin headlights, while cast-alloy wheels and dual front discs were specified. The finish was in black, with red side flashes and gold lining, while the wheels were gold anodised, so the appearance was striking.

In the middle of the year, Triumph produced another limited-edition Bonneville, this time to celebrate the marriage of Prince Charles to Lady Diana. Both USA and UK editions were built, with only 250 of the latter. The machine was called the Royal and based on the T140ES, but with twin Bing carburettors. The UK models had Morris cast-alloy wheels with twin discs, but for the

For the USA, the Royal Bonneville of 1981 had its own style of seat, tank and bars as well as a different finish.

The 649 cc TR65T Tiger Trail was very similar to the larger version but gained a heat shield for the silencer.

USA, wire wheels and one disc were thought adequate.

For the home market, the Royal had a silver-grey frame, matt black engine and fork sliders, and chrome-plated petrol tank with painted panels. For the USA, the petrol tank was smaller, but in the same plated finish, while the engine and fork legs were polished, and the frame black. Both types had new dualseats, the USA version being in the 'king and

Eight-valve cylinder heads had existed for Triumphs for some time but the 1982 TSS was the first to use one made by the firm itself.

queen' style to a limited extent. All the machines were numbered and certified.

There were additions to the range for 1982, and the first to appear was the TR65T Tiger Trail, which was much as its larger cousin. It used the engine from the Thunderbird, with a lower compression ratio, and kept the points ignition at first. The

discs as one for the TR65.

Two new models appeared for 1982, and one of them, the TSS, was equipped with an eight-valve engine and all-alloy top half. Inside, there was a new crankshaft with larger-diameter big-end journals of reduced width, which resulted in a stiffer component that was less prone to vibration. The machine was based

Engine unit of the TSS which was much as the stock T140 but had a stiffer crankshaft as well as the all-alloy top half.

cycle side was as for the TR7T, except for an additional heat shield on the silencer.

The three T140 models, the TR65 and the two trail machines ran into 1982 without the Royal. All had wire spoke wheels and a single disc front brake as standard, the cast-alloy wheels and dual discs being options for any of the T140 models. The electric starter continued as an option for the T140E, and the dual

on the TS8-1, but the special styling was no longer a feature, and the cycle side was mainly stock T140 with revised side covers and Marzocchi rear units. Twin 34 mm Amal Concentrics fed the engine with mixture, and the compact combustion chamber that came from the narrow valve angle and flat-top pistons allowed the use of a 9.5:1 compression ratio. Twin front discs and wire spoke wheels were fitted as stan-

TRIUMPH T140 BONNEVILLE

dard, but the cast-alloy wheels were an option.

The second new model was the TSX, which was in the custom style, but based on the stock T140. The engine was standard, being fitted with Bing carburettors and plain megaphone silencers. Cast-alloy wheels were standard, but while the front remained at 19in., the rear was

shafts, four exhaust ports and an internal balancer. There were four exhaust pipes, but only two silencers. On the cycle side, the engine was used as a stressed frame member, and there were telescopic front forks, a monoshock rear, cast-alloy wheels, and disc brakes. A development engine was also on show, coded Diana, while the machine

The TSX was introduced alongside the TSS in a custom style with a stock engine, Bing carburettors and plain megaphone silencers.

down to 16 in., and the twin front discs were an option. To suit the image, a two-level dualseat was fitted, along with high bars and a small petrol tank.

The firm's financial situation continued to be marginal but, despite this, they exhibited a new twin early in 1983. It was a prototype, so was kept on a plinth out of reach, but it featured water cooling, eight valves, chain-driven twin overhead cam-

itself was named the Phoenix 900.

The range for 1983 was announced at that show, but it was minus the two trail models, which had been dropped as sales had been poor. Also out were the T140E and Executive Bonneville, leaving only the T140ES in UK and USA forms. Both reverted to a 7 in. drum rear brake and had wire wheels with a single disc front brake. The twin discs continued to be an option, but

The Phoenix 900 whose twin overhead camshaft, watercooled, twin cylinder, eight-valve engine was coded 'Diana'.

not the cast-alloy wheels. All models lost their kickstart, so they had to rely on the electric foot.

For the UK model, the tyre diameters remained as they were, but the section of the rear one changed to 4.25 in. That model had the footrests moved back, so the gear pedal was given a new mounting in the primary chaincase to match and was connected to its original shaft by a remote linkage. A moulded tail went behind the seat but, in general, it was the Bonneville of old. The finish was in black, with a red flash or gold line, or in burgundy, all with stainless mudguards.

The USA version of the T140ES changed to a 16 in. rear wheel and had a dualseat with handrail behind it, rather than a tail. The handlebars were higher and the tank smaller than for the UK, but otherwise the models were the same with a similar finish. The main colour for the tank and side covers was black, Midnight blue or burgundy, but the side flash was multi-coloured, although the discreet gold lining was also available with the black.

Both the TSS and TSX continued, the former being available in the standard frame or the one with anti-vibration engine mountings. The TSS retained the cast-alloy wheel option and kept its dual front and single rear disc brakes. It received the same tyre section, revised footrest position, gear pedal linkage and seat tail as the UK version of the T140ES, and was listed in the same range of finishes.

The TSX was given the option of the eight-valve, all-alloy engine, but with a lower compression ratio, and its finish was as for the USA Bonneville. It kept the cast-alloy wheels as standard, and twin front discs as an

For its final 1983 year the T140ES Bonneville was shown with a drum rear brake in place of the long serving disc.

option, the models being badged TSX4 or TSX8, depending on the engine fitted. Except for the wheels, the first was the T140ES in USA form.

Two new models were added to the range for 1983, although few, if any, were to be built and sold. Both had a smaller, 599 cc, engine, and they were listed as the Daytona 600 and Thunderbird 600. The smaller capacity came by reducing the stroke to 66 mm, and the models were effectively the UK and USA Bonnevilles respectively in specification and colour. This included the twin front disc option, and the

only real divergence from this was that the Thunderbird had a single carburettor.

It was a last gallant attempt, but the money ran out. Motorcycle production had actually ceased in January 1983, and numerous attempts to interest backers had not met with success. In August, the firm went into voluntary liquidation, and towards the end of the year the stock, spares, tools and machinery were sold off. Shortly afterwards, the famous Triumph factory was demolished, a sad end after over 40 years of producing fine motorcycles.

Down in Devon

The closure of Meriden should have been the end of Triumph, but the name refused to lay down and be buried. The manufacturing rights were bought by businessman John Bloor, and he licensed Racing Spares to produce the Bonneville for five years.

Racing Spares was run by Les Harris to produce parts for Norton, BSA and Triumph at a factory in Bedfordshire, and he had been doing that for two decades. In their later days, the Meriden workforce had condemned him for taking profitable spares business from them, but the events of 1983 left him in the best position to move on from spares to complete machines.

Harris chose to set up his production line in Devon, and this took some time, as many of the traditional British suppliers were no longer in the motorcycle business. Thus, the brakes were Brembo, forks Paioli and the instruments Veglia.

The machine he was to build was, by agreement, the Bonneville in its final form and without any major changes. This was to allow Bloor freedom to plan a new factory on a green-field site, in which he intended to produce a new Triumph multi. The form this was to take was kept well under wraps, and it was 1989 before any real news emerged. Even this was limited, but suggested three or four cylinders, twin overhead

A 1983 newcomer was this 599 cc Thunderbird which duplicated the Bonneville in fitting a 16 in. rear wheel for its USA specification.

The UK version of the 599 cc machine was the Daytona which retained twin carburettors, unlike the Thunderbird.

camshafts, four valves per cylinder and water cooling. All far removed from the traditional Bonneville.

It was 1985 before the Devon-built twins reached the public and, under the licensing agreement, they were very much as the last Meriden Bonneville in UK and USA styles. About the only differences between the two were the handlebar rise and

Timing side of the Daytona with British lines but an older USA tank style in this case.

For 1983 the TSS, and others, had a remote gearchange as the footrests were moved back for easier high-speed riding.

tank capacity, for even the finish was common to both, in black with a red flash or gold lining for the tank and stainless-steel mudguards.

The power unit was the familiar 744 cc twin with five-speed gearbox, but without the electric starter and remote gear linkage. The twin Amal carburettors were Mark 1½ Concentrics, which were the original instrument fitted with the later cold-start system. In this form, they lost an annoying hesitation on acceleration, to which they had been prone.

The cycle side was as before, with the oil carried in the frame, twin rear units and slimline telescopic front forks. Both wheels had wire spokes and the traditional 19 in. front and

18 in. rear rims, while both had disc brakes with dual discs at the front.

Thus, the Bonneville lived on for a little longer and met with a favourable reception when first launched. The machine had its own niche in the market where its lines, stretching back some half a century, were familiar, while the performance was all about low- and mid-range torque, easy handling and highway or byway cruising. The footrests continued to be too far forward and inhibited high-speed motorway cruising, but that was not what the Bonneville was about.

The Triumph came from an era when even dual-carriageways were none too plentiful and often punctu-

Final 1983 version of the police Bonneville with its fairing, single seat and extra equipment for its duties.

ated with roundabouts. Elsewhere, the main roads wound their way through countryside and town, up hill and down dale. This placed a premium on crisp acceleration, good low-down power and a smart gearchange, all of which the Triumph twin offered.

The Devon-built Bonneville was never sold in the USA, due to the need for expensive product liability insurance to cover both Harris and Bloor. The machines were able to meet the USA emission requirements, Harris wished to sell, and customers wished to buy but, sadly, it was not to be. A generation had grown up with the notion that the

Devon Bonneville out on test where it proved to behave much as they always had.

The USA version of the Devon Bonneville which differed only in the handlebar rise and tank capacity from its home market brother.

answer to trouble was to sue, and the lawyers promoted this for all it was worth. No longer would riders admit that they might have made a mistake, and the net result was a prohibitive insurance premium.

By 1988, other factors began to have an effect. The original agreement was fast approaching its renewal date, and there was a suspicion that Bloor would not extend it, but launch his new Triumph, Harris having kept the name alive for him in the meantime. Next were some even tighter emission and noise regulations, which an air-cooled engine was unlikely to meet. Finally, the stock of crankcases was running low, and a new batch represented a large investment.

Taking all these factors into con-sideration produced the sensible commercial decision to cease production of the Bonneville. Harris had, by that time, revived the Matchless name for a machine powered by a 500 cc Rotax engine, and he chose to concentrate on that.

Thus, the Bonneville was finally laid to rest in 1988, some 30 years after it had made its T120 debut. During that time, it had seen great changes in the industry, but for much of the period, it had been THE machine to own. It continued to be prominent in the classic revival of the 1980s and, who knows, might yet make another Phoenix-like appearance in the decade to come. Whether it does or not, it will always have a significant place in motorcycling's history.

Triumph T140 Specifications

All models have two cylinders, overhead valves, five-speed gearbox, 12 volt electrics, telescopic front forks and pivoted-fork rear suspension. Petrol tank capacities are given for both UK and USA builds.

Model	T140V	TR7V	Jubilee	T140D	T140E	T140PE
years	1973-78	1973-81	1977	1979-80	1978-82	1980
bore mm	76[1]	76	76	76	76	76
stroke mm	82	82	82	82	82	82
capacity cc	744[1]	744	744	744	744	744
comp. ratio	8.25[2]	8.25[2]	7.9	7.9	7.9	7.9
carb type	930	930	930	930	930 Mk2	930 Mk2
carb size	30 mm	30 mm	30 mm	30 mm	30 mm	30 mm
top gear	4.7	4.7	4.7	4.7	4.7	
petrol - gall	4/3	4/3[3]	4/3	4/2	4/3[4]	3
front tyre	3.25x19	3.25x19	4.10x19	4.10x19	3.25x19[5]	3.00x19
rear tyre	4.00x18	4.00x18	4.10x18	4.10x18	4.00x18[5]	5.10x16
front brake dia	10 disc	10 disc	10 disc	10 disc	10 disc	10 disc
rear brake dia	7 drum[6]	7 drum[6]	10 disc	10 disc	10 disc	10 disc
wheelbase in.	56	56	56	56	56	

[1] - early-75mm and 725cc
[2] - 1976-7.9
[3] - 1976-4 only
[4] - 1981-4/2.3
[5] - 1979-4.10 section
[6] - 1976-10 disc

Triumph T140 Specifications

Model	T140ES	Executive	Royal	TR65	TR7T	TR65T
years	1980-83	1980-82	1981	1981-82	1981-82	1982
bore mm	76	76	76	76	76	76
stroke mm	82	82	82	71.5	82	71.5
capacity cc	744	744	744	649	744	649
comp. ratio	7.9	7.9	7.9	8.6	7.4	7.5
carb type	930 Mk2	930 Mk2[1]	Bing	930	930	930
carb size	30 mm	30 mm[1]		30 mm	30 mm	30 mm
top gear	4.7[2]	4.7	4.7	4.95	5.22	5.22
petrol - gal	4/2[3]	4	4/2.3	4/2.3	2.3	2.3
front tyre	4.10x19[4]	4.10x19	4.10x19	3.25x19	3.00x21	3.00x21
rear tyre	4.10x18[5]	4.10x18	4.10x18	4.00x18	4.00x18	4.00x18
front brake dia	10 disc	10 disc	10 disc	10 disc	10 disc	10 disc
rear brake dia	10 disc[6]	10 disc	10 disc	7 drum	7 drum	7 drum
wheelbase in.	56	56	56	56	56	56

[1] - 1981-Bing 32 mm
[2] - 1983-UK 4.48
[3] - 1981-4/2.3, 1983-USA 2.8
[4] - 1983-USA MJ90x19
[5] - 1983-UK 4.25x18, USA MT90x16
[6] - 1983-7 drum

Triumph T140 Specifications

Model	TSS	TSX	T'bird	Daytona	Devon
years	1982-83	1982-83	1983	1983	1985-88
bore mm	76	76	76	76	76
stroke mm	82	82	66	66	82
capacity cc	744	744	599	599	744
comp. ratio	9.5	7.4[1]	8.4	8.4	7.9
carb type	934 Mk2	Bing	930	930	Amal
carb size	34 mm	32 mm	30 mm	30 mm	Mk $1\frac{1}{2}$
top gear	4.48	4.7	4.95	4.95	4.7
petrol - gall	4	2.3[2]	2.8	4	4/2.8
front tyre	4.10x19	MJ90x19	MJ90x19	4.10x19	100/90x19
rear tyre	4.10x18[3]	MT90x16	MT90x16	4.25x18	110/90x18
front brake dia	10 disc	10 disc	10 disc	10 disc	10 disc
rear brake dia	10 disc	10 disc	7 drum	7 drum	10 disc
wheelbase in.	56	56	56	56	56

[1] - 1983-8.5 for TSX8
[2] - 1983-2.8
[3] - 1983-4.25x18